Day Begins When Darkness Is in Full Bloom

Poems by
Loretta Diane Walker

BLUE LIGHT PRESS ◆ 1ST WORLD PUBLISHING

BLUE LIGHT PRESS
1ST WORLD
PUBLISHING

SAN FRANCISCO ◆ FAIRFIELD ◆ DELHI

Day Begins When Darkness Is in Full Bloom

BLUE LIGHT PRESS
www.bluelightpress.com
bluelightpress@aol.com

1ST WORLD PUBLISHING
PO Box 2211
Fairfield, IA 52556
www.1stworldpublishing.com

BOOK & COVER DESIGN
Melanie Gendron
melaniegendron.com

COVER ART
"Nocturne" © by Meg Reilly

AUTHOR PHOTO
by Jessica Dominguez

FIRST EDITION

Library of Congress Cataloging-in-Publication Data

ISBN: 978-1-4218-3710-9

Praise for
Day Begins When Darkness Is in Full Bloom

In her powerful new collection of poems, *Day Begins When Darkness Is in Full Bloom*, Loretta Diane Walker takes us on harrowing journey, authenticated by striking and imaginative attentions—a testament to the strength of one woman's spirit faced with adversity, "the colliery of darkness," both physical and emotional, personal and cultural, local and historical. The range of these poems far exceeds their considerable force as personal narrative alone. "The sky is a mortuary for stars," she writes. "A lone bulb attempts to touch its round shadow." Here we find the play of a mercurial mind whose sober confrontation with mortality, illness, and marginalization moves seamlessly, with lyric inflection, toward understanding, affirmation, and an inclusiveness of vision and heart. A remarkable achievement.

— Bruce Bond

I am lucky to have met and heard Loretta Diane Walker read her poems on many occasions, so when I was reading this collection, I listened for a voice I knew well: a soft, precise lament, on the edge of tears, drenched continually by unexpected pain and grief, yet still rising again and again to the light of hope, most evident in what I have always admired in her craft, the original metaphor, unique to the poem, and to me, yet still apt, piercing in truth, shining like a familiar star in the ink of the night, just like, as she writes, the "faces of angels you can only see in darkness."

— Laurence Musgrove, author of *Local Bird* and
The Bluebonnet Sutras, editor of *Texas Poetry Assignment*.

I love these poems, these calculations of hope that emerge from *a colliery of darkness* fueled by cancer, racism, the pandemic and loss. I love how Loretta Diane Walker wrestles with the world as it is and emerges again and again with clear, rich poems that *wash the soul in light*. This is a collection of healing and hard-won hope. It opened me.

— Rosemerry Wahtola Trommer, author of *Hush* and *Naked for Tea*

The poems in *Day Begins When Darkness Is in Full Bloom* are informed by a deep grieving for both the lyric speaker's own personal suffering, and that of our larger world. We see in Loretta Walker's richly imagist poems human suffering in its many forms — whether that be one's growth into adulthood without the presence of a faithful parent, or the pain and uncertainty of a cancer patient's ongoing treatment, or the challenges each of us now face daily as we live in the midst of a global pandemic, or the individual and social turmoil engendered by racial bigotry, and its consequent injustices. Walker's is a necessary grief. It is the transformation of that grieving that leads her to the balm of the natural world, and the predictable cycle of seasons tethering us to the earth. The book's arc leads both poet and reader to praise this life, to celebrate the time we each have in our world — the poems themselves enacting survival, salvation.

— Robin Davidson

Author's Note

I don't want to write about the bucket of darkness I brought with me into this pandemic. It wasn't my choice; circumstance beyond my control flooded into my life.

I don't want to write about when I was so tired, I could hardly get out of bed, or when I was so weak, I wet my pajamas on the way to the bathroom, or that ninety-five percent of the time I still sleep in my clothes.

I don't want to write about a physical pain so unbearable I called 911 and agreed to go to a place where COVID-19, according to the paramedics, "is active."

I don't want to write about the ER doctor, after various scans, announcing apologetically that cancer tumors fractured my spine — my first hospital stay. Two of the nurses that cared for me were former students. One of them removed her mask, put her face next to mine, with our tears fusing, she promised to take care of me.

I do not want to write about the residual pain that still haunts me, even after radiation started the process of knitting my spine back together.

I don't want to write that my younger sister can't stand to see my bedroom door closed because she heard a loud thud, found me on the floor, passed out, due to large blood clots in my lungs. She held me, rocked me, begged me to stay with her. I heard my brother-in-law speaking to the 911 operator as he told her each time I took a breath. I tell them, "I'm tired." When I woke up, clothes cut from my body, I found myself in the ER once again. That time I spend two days in ICU with instructions not to move my right leg.

I don't want to write about the month it took for the insurance company to approve crucial life-saving medication because my out-of-pocket portion was too high.

I do not want to write about the fear that hovers around the edges of my psyche, but each event is a part of my pandemic reality.

However, I do want to write, after two hospital stays, I spend my time shuffling between doctor appointments, the oncology center for treatments, and reconciling my spirituality, as well as my mortality.

A new cancer diagnosis, just six months after I was in remission for the second time, causes me to reevaluate the way I view life in general and fills me with gratitude. I still cry about the diagnosis, but am grateful for the kindness and love family and friends pour into my life.

Each day I cherish my sister and brother-in-law for taking me in, to care for me as I grow strong enough to care for myself. I do not regard any gestures of kindness as "small." I cherish every get-well card, offerings of prayer, comfort, encouragement, phone calls, text messages, flowers, meals, emails, books, and other surprises I receive via postal mail. This speaks volumes of the people I have in my life; in the midst of their challenges, they make strong efforts to keep my spirits lifted.

When I wrote "Will We Still Desire Touch?" I had no idea at the time how desperate I would desire touch and how grateful I would be to receive it. During my second hospital stay, after I was moved from the ICU unit to a private room, I broke down and cried uncontrollably.

The hospital halls were eerily quiet, footsteps echoed if a person wore shoes without a soft sole. It was Mother's Day, and I was alone. A young nurse on the late shift entered my room to check on me. When she discovered I was crying, she asked, *What's the matter?*

When I could not verbalize my emotions, she began to stroke my hair as if I were her child. She spoke words I had one time rebuked, but that night, those exact words became a healing balm. She said, *I always tell my mother God will not give you more than you can handle. You can handle this.* She continued to stroke my hair until I started to drift off to sleep.

I wear my pink hospital "limb alert" band until it fades — a reminder of the miracles and events that led up to healing and the emotional and spiritual growth I am experiencing.

This book is dedicated to my family
who opened their lives to me —
James Walker, Chris and Lisa Walker,
Vincent and Earnestine Walker, Mark, Kim, and
Jamarkus Schiff, and to the memories of
Mary A. Walker and Raymond Walker.

Gratitude

I want to take this time to thank:

…Diane Frank and Blue Light Press for publishing this book.

…Melanie Gendron, book designer.

…Diandra Walker Robertson for the author photo.

…Meg Reilly for the cover photo.

… Bruce Bond, Laurence Musgrove, Rosemerry Wahtola Trommer, and Robin Davidson for their gracious endorsement of this collection.

…Barbara Blanks for devoting so much of herself and time editing and discussing these poems.

…Cindy Huyser for the late-night conversations concerning this collection.

…My circle of friends who supported me as If I were family.

… Pankaj Khandelwal, M.D., Joseph Kaczor, M.D., Sissy A. Hinojos, MPAS, PA-C, Ryan C. Sperl, MPAS, PA-C, Matthew B. Furst, M.D., Faye Armstrong-Paap, M.D., and the staff at Texas Oncology-Odessa West Texas Cancer Center for their impeccable care.

…My Reagan Magnet School Family

…My Wagner Noel Family

…My Blue Light Press Family

Acknowledgments

Amulet Poetry Magazine

Beautiful Cadaver Pittsburg Project: Is It Hot in Here or Is It Just Me?

Black Dog & One-Eyed Press

Blues and the Blues Anthology

The Blue Hole Anthology

A Book of the Year: The Poetry Society of Texas

Boundless: Rio Grande Valley International Poetry Festival Anthology

Cathexis Northwest Press

Conceit Magazine

Conestoga Zen

Concho River Review

Connecticut River Review

Ekphrastic Review

Encore Prize Poems

Equinox

Gasconade Review #5

Langdon Review of the Arts in Texas

Langdon Review of the Arts in Texas TEJASCOVIDO Edition

Lone Stars 93 Anthology

Lucy Writers Platform: Cambridge

Melting Pot Anthology

The Monterey Poetry Review

Pandemic Puzzle Poems Anthology

Table of Contents

Part One: Diagnosis

Epistle 1:

Imagine this scenario: June — after reviewing results of both my mammogram and blood work, the oncologist announced I was in remission. October — after having reconstruction surgery I was told, "You have cancer." November — I had a mastectomy and was told all of the cancer is gone. April — for two weeks I experienced excruciating unending pain which prompted a trip to the emergency room. I was told a tumor fractured my spine and I had cancer.

For months I told people I was "fine" or "okay." There were times I screamed in my pillow to prevent my neighbors, sister, and brother-in-law from hearing me. Although my soul was saturated with tears, there were times I was in so much pain I could not cry.

I use the word "tears" several times in this section. Those tears I could not bring forth surfaced here; I inevitably began crying on these pages.

Cancer is a crooked road without signs,
where the ground shifts without warning…
— Carey Link

Earthquakes, COVID, and Cancer

Spring's flora takes roll call of its colors:
honeysuckle yellow, camellia pink, primrose purple.

The earth quakes in this desert city of Odessa.

Curious how fissures in Mother Earth's womb
cause her to suddenly shake.
The tremors are like tumors,

2.5, 2.8, 3.2.
Curious unlike Carole King

I don't *feel the earth move*
under my feet or feel the sky
come tumbling down
when the emergency room doctor
in his sympathetic syrupy Dr. Pepper
voice says, *I'm sorry. You have cancer.*
The tumor has fractured your spine.
Shock is a mammoth hand over my mouth,
smothers breaths I try to exhale.
My cries fall into a tangled net of silence.

In that sanitized room where walls cannot chart
the height of sun, or measure the speed of the wind as it trots
in colorless tennis shoes,
hear the syncopated rhythms of feathers and leaves
as grackles fly in and out of trees,
I have become a queen bee without her loyal hive.

Such loneliness when I fly into a world
where the no in normal is a dictator:

no handshakes,
no swirl and spin
of schoolyard merry-go-rounds,
no naked faces swimming in oceans of air,
where an ambulance siren wails
when pain and blood clot my lungs and my back.

But the way paramedics lift, transport,
my body's pained cargo, the way my blouse is cut,
ripped from me like a soiled past,

the way a young nurse who once called me teacher,
leans her maskless face against mine,
the liquid of our eyes flowing together like one river,
are my love letters from God.

Variation on Cancer Blues

8:27 a.m.
Trains of cool air barrel through a dark subway
of clouds this October morning.
I walk beneath the subtle rumble of wind,
hands tucked in my pockets,
gait a cross between leap and slow trot
through double doors of a black plexiglass medical building.
My sister trails behind,
care heavy on her shoulder.
"Slow down," her words a caution sign.
Awaiting celebration, I forget the bloody steri-strips,
slightly soiled bandages, tight bra that binds my new breasts —
the roundness of pain that fills them.
The drain, attached like an appendage
for the last six days, is scheduled for amputation.
In anticipation, I move my fingers up then down
my thighs the way I do when warming up on my saxophone.

8:40 a.m.
The surgeon says, "On the count of three, take a deep breath."
The launch pad of his voice gentle, "1. 2. 3."
I inhale, feel the stingy snip of scissors, a sudden yank
the long skinny rubber hose exodus from my body.
Why is freedom so painful?

8:47 a.m.
After rattling off a litany of instructions to my sister
for wound care, the surgeon slouches in a corner chair.
I read his eyes like a jazz chart.
His pupils, typically quick riffs of joy,
are sad measures of rests.
So many I lose track of the melody.

My ears drop more words than they catch.

"We sent…Lab found…. Small…. Cancer."

Second diagnosis.

Once, I believed hope came between that stretch
of emptiness between dreams and waking.
Now, I believe it's the space between a blink.
When it comes, I treat it like a new lover.
If not, I might snap the one delicate string
that will hold me together.

The Night Before Surgery

I walk through an archway of doors.
The sun, an open wound, bleeds heat.
Angst is another name for tree.

Tumors are the hard terrain of fear.
Fear is a flowerless forest.
Blood does not flower when needles prick.

My throat is a pink dried river.
I walk through sunlit doors
into a forest without red.

Consent Form

From the whirlpool of nausea and anesthesia,
a doctor said my name, Loretta, Loretta, Loretta,
unstopped the mass of silence that plugged my ears.

Two blood-and fluid-filled drains
hung from my faux right breast.
When day was still called morning,

I signed my name on a consent form,
gave the hospital permission
to dispose of my breast as they saw fit.

Mastectomy. Amputation. What's the difference?
How does one armor oneself against such loss?
Tattoo the shoulders with dragonflies?
Dance in a slow mist of rain?

I cried.
Sobs dropped hard into the cistern of my pillow.
My loss — a burdened ox, carried what was still wanted.

During the fragile hours between dusk and dawn,
I prayed, give this cancer, rooted like milkweed,
wings.

From the blue darkness, a west Texas wind chanted
my prayers back to me.
I watched as stars mouthed in their distant light,

healing was in the blood and in the cutting.

When I Lost My Hair: In Four Movements

I

The scissors' biting blades were strangers
to my panda-colored kinky thatch.
Seven years it grew like wildflowers.

II

I pulled patches from my itchy scalp,
tufts filled the pouch of my surprised hand.
Chemoed-hair — black tears in a white sink.

III

The comb raked more loosened locks like leaves.
A colorful scarf bound what remained.
Grief fitted in the folds of fabric.

IV

Clippers buzzed and hummed a requiem.
Hair fell like wrong notes onto the floor.
My head — *Bald Symphony in B-Minor.*

Chemo Session Number Eighteen

tastes like session twelve.
Feels like session five.
Sounds like session seven.
Smells like session six.
Looks like session eight.

Prick skin. Inhale. Exhale. Draw blood.
Connect port. Recite birthday.
Link: anti-nausea and steroids,
Benadryl and Pepcid,
chemo cocktail and saline rinse bags —

plastic ropes dangle from a pole
with a singing timer.

Each Thursday I rehearse the same
ceremonial treatments in the chemo room.
Each Thursday the leaves of faces change,
except for Mr. Lopez. He is a branch
hanging by the window.

I drift into sleep as chemical sap flows
through the trunk of my body.
A mechanical voice lilts "do," "re," "mi"
in the key of "A Flat Major," wakes me.
Flat empty bags. Tokens of proof

I lived through another Thursday, walk out into a day
where the sky doesn't bother to change its afternoon shirt.

The Fruit of Trust

I examine trust, that delicate translucent fruit,
from the platter of my palm,
cannot remember how many times I turn it over
before taking a dainty bite.
The tangy-sweet flavor dissolves
in my musky mouth when I lean my head
into the chest of a young nurse with her face masked.
Her beaver-colored eyes look down at me
from behind a veil of long dark lashes
as she strokes my unkempt hair with blue gloves —
her voice a lullaby as my weeping salts my unwashed face.
Maybe because it's Mother's Day,
maybe because she is a mother,
maybe because she feels I am motherless
she comforts me as a child.
On the edge of sleep, I hear her shut the door
to my hospital room with its walls white as bread.
Admonished to keep my right leg still,
I roll my head to the left, pray
I will wake to see that suction cup of sun
sip out night's last dark breath.

A Doctor's Touch

for Doctors Armstrong, Furst,
Kaczor, Khandelwal, and O'Hearn

Your hands are chameleons.
Probe in search of cells clumped like grapes
hiding beneath this vine of skin.
Lifeboats sailing over this dark sea of flesh
in search of a disease docked in the cave of my breast.
Wolves hunting prey hidden in the den of my body.

Grief is a chameleon too.
A pillowcase snug on my head.
Rolls of saran wrap wrapped around
me from crown to sole, sealing fresh pain
with each labored breath.
Nacre in the belly of an oyster.

My right breast, an apparition,
drifts through a cupola of surgical lights.

This winter morning an untamed quiet
is rampant throughout the streets
and snow is a six-inch top hat
snug on this desert city.
I am a chameleon too —
the naked fruitless mulberry in my backyard.
Every exposed limb and branch are the arms
of those who lifted me from a colliery of darkness.

When I Pray This Morning

I am a broken-winged robin hiding in a dry meadow
with fall's crisp leaves crunching beneath my feet.

Is it a good thing to have chosen such a small
wounded body to imagine myself in?

For weeks my family and friends are crutches.
My thoughts and prayers are with you they say.

I am cancer's prey, bound with dependence.
I glance at my neighbor from my office window,

feel jealousy towards her freedom sneaking
into my traumatized body.

She cradles an e-cigarette in the corner
of her mouth like a 1930's movie star.

As she puts her vehicle in reverse, backs into the abyss
of day, smoke drifts from her mouth like incense.

A blood-red scarf hangs from a fencepost.
The altar of tall pickets intimidating as fear.

In the distance, I hear an ambulance's siren.
This is how some prayers are answered

I supposed — with wailing and flashing lights.

I hold a hot cup of tea; the smoky images of my hands
cover the constant incantation of crying.

My Therapist Said, If You Want to Heal, Stay Off Facebook,
My Oncologist Agreed

More words than faces storm pages with quelling waves
of pessimism/optimism, devotion/disdain —
the yin & yang of ourselves.
Seventy days I heed both doctors' advice,
become a beadless woman,
ride a translucent horse into distances,
the future an impressionist painting hanging
in the corridor of my life.

Drowning in ennui, I return to Facebook,
wet with anticipation.
When I scan the horizon, my eyes fixate on
Today the whole world is the same age.
Today is a very special day…
To calculate, add your age plus your year of birth.
I sit at the kitchen table, scratch the equation —
2020+age+birth year on a soiled sheet of typing paper,
get an answer of 40.
Do the equation again with a calculator,
then compile the age and birthdate of old lovers,
siblings, friends. Same answer.
What of this planet with its 7.7 billion people?
How do you reduce a sundry of souls to double digits?
Make us the same?

This is how I calculate hope:
the fractured spine will fuse, heal after radiation,
the tumors will shrink into nothingness,
the cancer will leave my body forever,
too repulsed by my faith to return.

This is what I dream:
the giant blow-up doll tethered to a post
in front of the Fast Signature Loans building
is a freed bald eagle.
Sharp daggers of grass slice through my belly
clustered with stars.
I bleed light.

How Not to Fail Babysitting 101

There are no flies in Goshen
and no nuts in this jar of peanut butter
my nephew will not eat from.
His rather — Mentos.
With knees to carpet, he sings *Fernando*
as he sketches the shape of Alaska from memory.
He is an image of faith,
a wonder who becomes more precious each day.

His soft coiled locks too sandy for blonde.
Skin too pale for black, too dark for white.
A shade many enslaved black girls birthed.
His mother comes from the lineage of Sheba,
his father from David.

His mind is a vault.
Words, numbers, shapes, colors,
people, places, the small bites
of this world that fit in his eyes and ears
are locked inside.
I want to open him up, be a voyeur
inside his beautiful mind.
What if the pitcher of myself cannot hold
all he has to pour into me?

His lanky fingers smell of black Sharpie.
These same inky hands helped nurse me back to health
when his mother and father took me in for almost a year,
cared for me when sleep came in the form of pain pills,
when I was too weak to walk, eat, drink,
when cancer wrestled me twice more.
His voice, once my melodic alarm clock,

now a megaphone packed with warning
when I pick up the remote,
"Put that remote down."
In an embarrassed tone I respond,
"Don't you want to watch Flea Market Flip?"

His left hand is a crane as he lifts the remote
from a green decorative bowl shaped like an opened rose,
places it on a clean sheet of typing paper, glances at me,
"We don't watch television when we work."
I return to a manuscript, attempt to airbrush it with metaphors.
Ten minutes later I rake my eyes across the room.
They pause at a replica of the remote etched on typing paper.
Each button thick with precision and ink.
He hums *Fernando*.
I think— there are no flies in Goshen.

Triple Crown

As the world keeps stepping away from itself,
I want to kiss this purple web
of bruised veins in the fold of my left arm
and the needle pricks in my left fingers
where gloved hands touch.
I feel their lives pulsing
as they draw the flow of life from me.
Is it madness to rejoice in this pain, the feel of latex,
the medley—blood pressure, temperature, meds?
Insanity to give gratitude for this fracture,
slowed gait, ticks of pain, dehydrated tears,
and third cancer prognosis?
Conceit to desire a triple crown
of remission?

I do not want to shut myself inside myself
as the world keeps stepping away from itself.
Outside my window I listen to:
my neighbor's weights clash against each other
as he lifts and curses with labored breath,
a small convention of birds
rehearse warbles and coos,
accompanying their melodies with wingbeats
against new branches
as swells of hope pour into the country of my body.
Even disease cannot drive it out.

Part Two: Grief

Epistle 2:

July 2013 is when I was first diagnosed with stage two breast cancer. I had a lumpectomy, twenty sessions of chemotherapy, and thirty-seven sessions of radiation therapy. I took hormone blockers for five years to continue the treatment. June 2019 both my mammogram and bloodwork came back cancer free. I was officially in remission. For this reason, I decided to have breast reconstruction to repair the damage to my right breast. September 10, thirty days before the surgery, I received news my eldest brother, Raymond Walker, died suddenly from complications of stage four prostate cancer. His death came on the heels of my mother's death one year prior. February 2021, Katie Arnold, my mother's eldest sister and best friend, passed from this life. Auntie, as my siblings and I fondly addressed her, was a surrogate mother.

Because of my breast cancer history, tissue samples were sent to the lab for testing. During the follow-up office visit, the surgeon informed me they found a small cancer cell in my right breast. After consulting with the oncologist, he said, "Your only option to live is a mastectomy." Earlier in that week, I promised a dear friend, a breast cancer survivor herself, and one who walked with me on my first journey, that I would text her after my appointment with the oncologist. Thirty minutes after I received the news, I sent a group text to her and two other friends. I immediately received a phone call after that text and was informed my friend, Dr. Tracie Gibson, had died. She is one of several friends I would lose.

On August 31, 2019, I received a frantic phone call from my sister, "Where are you?" she asked. I was standing outside my door, getting ready to lock it, "On my way to Dillard's." The urgency in her voice caused me to stop, "Listen to Earnie before you leave!" Earnie, my sister-in-law informed me about the shooting taking place in Odessa/Midland. I could hear sirens, but learned to tune them out because I live a mile from a fire station. "Turn on the news," my sister-in-law insisted. A gunman was on a shooting rampage. I live in the vicinity where residents were warned to stay indoors, less than a mile where some of the shooting took place. After the shooting spree was over, eight lives were lost and twenty-five people were injured. Sadly, some of those injured and one of the ones lost, were a part of my Reagan Elementary family.

So here I was faced with grief, upon grief, upon grief. My new journey, to wash my soul in light after it had plunged into the basement of darkness.

Before you know kindness as the deepest thing inside,
you must know sorrow as the other deepest thing.
— Naomi Shihab Nye

When Sirens Shatter the Air

When prayer claws through screams, makes its way
through the dark tunnel of a traumatized throat.
When silence is too heavy for the ears to carry.
When the heart only knows allegro as tempo.
When fear becomes flesh.
When shrapnel rips through innocence.
When CPR is a broken tool.
When lead takes a father, a child.
When windshields hold the memories
of sudden violence.
When the young press their faces
in a rough field for protection.
When the ones who vowed to save lives
hug the ones who vowed to protect lives.
When a hair-netted woman picks up
wet sorrow drowned in tissues.
When the pizza delivery guy delivers
sustenance to families with famished spirits.
When a community's blanket of security tatters.
When answers do not match questions.
When grief begets grief, and grief, and grief,
we reach for something, someone beyond ourselves.
Some call it hope.
Some call it love.
Some call for God.
In our blind reaching,
we write a message with our tears.
I don't want to be alone.
We are not alone.

Who Will Mourn with Your Mother?

"How does one make sense of having a child
who has killed several people?... Lanza, as Solomon wrote,
wished his son had never been born, explaining,
"That didn't come right away.
That's not a natural thing, when you're thinking about your kid..."
—Joe Pinsker, staff writer at "The Atlantic"

She lost you twice.
First to the grave of insanity.
Then to the shallow pools of your blood.

After the nurse handed you to your mother,
did she count your fingers and toes,
coo and cry, dream your future?

After she delivered you
into the universe's hands of light,
how could she have known

your cells would fill with darkness?
Mutate and mask the man
you were before you were no longer?
Curious how death requires only
the smallest of streams, tiniest of punctures
to mutilate a life beyond recognition.

This is selfishness.
This is truth.

I want a downpour of rain.
I don't want to hear the steady beat
of melancholy in wiper blades
as they swipe away sky's hard sobbing.

Its heavy tears the only compassion
she'll feel against her guilty cheeks.
The only absolution she'll receive

for your sins.

The Undertaker at the Colored Cemetery in McCamey, Texas

In your dome of grief,
is he your enemy or friend?
What is the breadth between the two
when death is the wedge?
Bless the hands
that attempt to preserve the shape of life
in a body whose soul skipped out
before it reached him.
Who knows where a spirit plods
when it takes off life's apron?
What devotion from a man
who met you two days ago,
the way he stands beneath this canopy
in his dark suit, its flimsy cloth not cushioned
enough to catch extravagant heat
as the sun plays fast-pitch baseball —
throws temperatures above ninety degrees.
Swatches of sweat cover
his strawberry-colored face
as ghosts of the past loiter
around traumatized mourners.
After the last rites, they depart —
spirits to a lone belt of cloud
stretched over the cemetery.
The undertaker strides down the caliche road
where dust and the sadness
of others settle on his polished black shoes.

Navigator

A eulogy poem for Raymond Walker

He was our GPS, our road map, our big brother.
Before Apple's seeds of cell phones,
before Garmin, TomTom, and Mio
became dashboard passengers,
phone booths, quarters, collect calls,
and other motorists' kindnesses
were our only roadside assistance plans.

He charted, with no alternate routes for detours,
our destinations in his bright blue ink.
Confident we'd arrive, wherever "there" is,
trusted we'd read, follow road signs, and steer
in directions he mapped out for us.

Our brother, a husband, a father, grandfather —
now navigates his life's legacies
with a new compass of love,
sets a course for them all to carry his name
into places he'll never visit.

Years travel through us like invisible roads.
We record them as if they are mile markers.
Who can trace the veins of distance on such roads?

His long slow smile, his love for speed,
and his sudden departure
is like pain on a red Bugatti, racing through us
so fast our tears cannot catch up.

But our hearts will keep reaching,
knowing we can still touch you
through the vehicle of memories.

Before I Knew You Were Gone

In memory of Dr. Tracie Gibson

I reach out to tell you this news,
my breasts are like the wings of a "v,"
lifted, ready for the launch, to land
in words like love, voice, vacant.

Before the anesthesiologist sent me
down the deep river of sleep
where there are no shadows or light,
only a shrine of darkness,
the surgeon drew a "v"
on the base of my neck.
A compass aimed in the direction
of reconstruction.
An unassuming explorer, he discovers cancer cells
hidden in old radiated chemoed flesh.

Cruelty, like hunger, is a constant in the universe.
What other word carries the punch of this sudden jolt?
Thirty minutes after I learn my breasts are the sacrifices
to maintain my life, I learn you died.
Dead two days before you're discovered.
Dead like my brother thirty days ago.

Where are the strong nets to hold this shock?
Bubbles of joy that rise up, rinse clean any sadness?
The bones of my resolve are breaking.

Desperate, I search for meaning in numbers:
two — union, separation. Thirty, blood.
Then think about a pair of swans I adored while in Houston.
The way their graceful long necks almost formed a heart.

The way the small space of distance between them
is like an open wound or a door
where lost things fall through, pass into the ether.
Like my amputated breasts and my mother's amputated legs.
Will they know each other?

I find two notes tucked inside a get-well card.
One with a large heart accenting the page,
both scribbled from the same six-year-old hand:
Dear Miss Walker I hope you are going to be ok love Addie.
Music is everything to me.

This is the meaning I gather from numbers:
when small things are larger than the universe
and morsels of light are as Deneb in the black hole
of my pain, perhaps it is hope.
Perhaps it is healing.

For Your Name Sake

In memory of Robin Gutierrez

The birds of the sky nest by the waters,
they sing among the branches. (PS 104:12).

Faith, that nail you hang
on the door of morning,
is your story.

Hope is the legs you use to walk into a day
filled with uncertainty. Grace the way
you flick trials away with your fingers.

You are song,
an anthem of light,
psalm of hope, hymn of grace.

Oh, the laughter you sing into the world.
Your voice echoes in lives,
moves them to excavate deeper

into that room
of self where the impossible
becomes possible.

You are the meaning of spring.
In the harshest of winters,
storms cannot blanket your smiles.

To Swallow Light

When death fed me darkness
for over a year, illuminated days
raged at love with excessive blue.
Lambent afternoon light
seemed to pout with such sadness
the wind mocked it with moaning.

The lengthy, hot shower, stifled with steam,
the thud and rattle of coffee mugs
crescendoing in the dishwasher's scald,
the ceaseless clunk of the washing machine
spinning from its balance — the melancholia
of the mundane.

The darker the horizon, the juicier the tears.
In the cell of my sadness, I cowered in my closet,
screamed until the gospel of my moans
echoed in my clothes,
fell asleep on the carpetless floor,
my throat clogged with fatigue and salt.

I woke, uncrumpled my stiff body
dragged myself to bed
where a humble pool of light streamed
from the small lamp on my nightstand.
With swollen eyes and aching head,
the thirty watts splattered in my dried mouth
as I switched off the lamp —
my heart roasting in the flames of grief.

Absolution

Memories, landmarks in the gray town of my mind
where urgent cries echo through sunless rooms:
my ten-year-old self obsessing over five cavities
and the silver mines they create in my mouth;
the milky haze from the roach bombs Mom ignites
before we move into a tiny apartment
with a sad sagging roof,
the unforgiving confessions of its creaky floors;
elders who sing Amen to wind, wounds, wounded-dreams
'cause history's ceremony grooms them to remain humble,
ask for nothing more than the poverty
spilling from the pockets of their second-hand cotton dresses.

Maybe I should confess
at age eleven, I threw rocks at two dogs sinning.
I was a bedwetter until age twelve.
In middle school, bonding with cool girls was fruitless.
I failed an English test so they would like me.
I tried a cigarette, choked, they still didn't like me.
I wanted to taste stars in the Milky Way,
curious of their sweetness.

Nineteen, I pressed a blade against my wrist,
didn't know the difference between a crocus and hyacinth.
The first time I had cancer, I prayed to die
after the fourth injection of the "red devil."
But the children kept singing in my head
until my body was song.
I slept. Wept. Lived
to plant a garden with sunflowers and begonias.

Time is a manipulator.
Why do I make these confessions to the sky now
on this sultry September day?
West Texas heat is unforgiving.
With no insult to butterflies, I stand beneath
a chestnut tree, snub their existence, long for
the hummingbird I saw yesterday,

and all the yesterdays

when my body was a stainless cathedral of health.

Vanish

And what do you say to the light
as it vanishes behind a stall of redwoods,
as the hem of its long skirt falls,
snags in a patch of unhewn ferns?

        The bees are disappearing.

And in the dusk-colored hours, do you hush
your beagle singing to strangers?
It is difficult for a dog's mirth to understand
its bark is not song.

        The northern white rhinos are disappearing.

How do you repair a day roaring with fear,
wildly giving way to impulse, ripping secrets
from the belly of mobile homes, flipping pickups like coins?

    Behind a dense drape of rain,
    people are disappearing.

And how do I tell death water is hope?
Last year a yellow calla lily returned
after I left it vulnerable in winter's harsh grip.
Perhaps all withering is not the end.

I dream: all those disappeared bees pollinating
fields filled with sunflowers and daises,
the horizon's distant breath
blowing locks of dandelion hair
like bubbles across the sky;
they fall on the white rhinos,

their wide mouths opened as the heavens pour
sunshine over their thick woundless skin,
and the people are in their houses,
lounging in easy-chairs,
their laughter blaring like rock & roll.

A thunderstorm charges from the east,
flings hail against my windows.
   Am I disappearing?

Ask

Ask children or birds what blackberries taste like.
Ask the frog why it never complains
about the temperature of the pond.
Ask the deer why it risks its life to return home.
Ask the eagle if its lonely to be majestic.
Ask the bald mulberry if it misses the fallen leaves.
Ask the blowing leaves if they grieve aged limbs.
Ask the spoon the flavor of my tongue.
Ask my bones if they desire strength or beauty.
Ask my blood if it wants to drip or flow.
Ask my lungs what is the meaning of air.

Sunflowers and Lilacs

For Katie Lorene Walker Arnold (Auntie), 1929-2021
"Katie was known for her enormous sunflowers and lilac wisteria."

Auntie, perhaps you are a seraph.
I am oblivious of your affairs and of time
where you are now.

In Odessa, it is June.
Early morning.
The moon and darkness refuse
to relinquish their shifts.
I am a sleepless salmon spawning
through Facebook feeds.
Click the heart emoji

for a mother and her trio of daughters
modeling matching sunflower outfits.
Their pose, pacific. Smiles luminous
beside an eight-foot sunflower.
I smile back at them

the way I do at your funeral.
Your grandson jokes,
"You know you are a Big Mama kid
when she coaxes a confession with poundcake."
He christens you a super hero,
brags you can spot a lie in a second,
see a wayward child down a forbidden street,
can decipher guilty body language,
stop a spat with a stare.

Auntie, perhaps you are a seraph.
I am oblivious of your affairs and of time
where you are now.

Days creep into weeks
before I return to Facebook.
The mother and her trio of daughters
modeling matching sunflower outfits,
ascend into the internet's translucent ether.
When February comes, we cover our bodies in lilac,
pin artificial sunflowers to our chests,
celebrate your life.

I read all life is doomed to death.
Meadow voles chirping in rough fields.
Flocks of sparrows flapping their shadows against the sky.
Colorful Koi flipping in a new backyard pond.
Each of us crying violeta and amarillo sadness
because your breath floated beyond Pluto
and never returned.

Part Three: Social Unrest during COVID

Epistle 3:

The murders of Breonna Taylor and George Floyd, the deep divide in our country, the insurrection and attack on our nation's capital, and the level of hatred "for the other," that derived during COVID became boils on my essence. My soul oozed with such sorrow, anger, and helplessness I struggled with words. There were days I refused to watch the news and abstained from social media for several weeks. However, when I thought I had cocooned myself from the ugliness, a group of Zoom Bombers disrupted a poetry reading and open mic by calling me a Nigger and other foul words. I was the only black person in the session; thus, the words were directed at me. It is disturbing to have offensive language hurled at you by strangers hidden behind a dark screen, but it is more disheartening when someone in local leadership flaunts a picture of a noose, and proudly posts a litany of derogatory statements aimed at various minority groups. The hate is no longer out there, but in your living-room, sitting in your lap.

Pain, that strong current, rips through the world,
its waves crushing as massive stones.

Ways of Looking at Your Hands
When COVID is the Conductor

Where is the woman in the long silk gown?
The one with rose-colored rouge on her face,
and a morning-colored diamond
winking from her right ear.
The one who chases music through millennia.

There's a concert in the small hall of my hands.
I perform on the two brown stages,
the dissonant music of splash and swish
as I robustly rub Dial antibacterial soap
into my skin.
The incessant washing and use of hand sanitizer
bleach my palms like O'Keefe's cow skulls,
exposes every line life has etched into my hands.
Once, I thought they were some instrument
of clutching and releasing.
Hands cannot be deceived.
They know the ritual of becoming.

Today I write the grackles' story —
the way they congregate before dawn
or after sunset on tree branches, wires or roofs,
fill the air with their song and caw.
Citizens scream for their silence and dissonance
but do not celebrate resilience
in their iridescent feathers.
They are blackbirds, too, just like me.
Am I afraid of my own story —
of the ones who despise my blackness?
Is resilience a weapon? A helmet? A fist?

I stare in the cup of my hands, see no shadows.
This hidden darkness is everything I want to crush.
I want to hold fast to every colorful thing
that makes me a black woman.

Witnessing the Lynching, from the Sky's Diary

"Negro Is Slain by Texas Posse: Victim's Heart Removed After His Capture By Armed Men" was published in The New York World Telegram on December 8, 1933

Account 1: Sky

Curses of the first born, the archivist of the all-in-all.
The receptacle of every act and uttered secret.
Born before time itself, I am predicated to this position
of witnessing hobbies of cruelty based on certain men
worshiping the pale pigmented temple of their skin.
Longevity is cruel; I can never unremember blood dripping
through history from frenzied clubs, lust-filled blades
for the taste of a negro's plasma and the long drop
and snap of a black life.

Account 2: Justice

Fashioned with fair hands to hold sword and scales,
balance morality, I am ignored.
Guilt, innocence tastes the same
on hate's singed tongue.
Truth is a nuisance;
accusations kindle for fires
to destroy what is different.
I am a blind amputated woman.

Account 3: The Rope

Beneath a jungle of stars, darkness stings with disdain.
I cradle an innocent neck, whisper I'm sorry, I'm sorry
as I look down at a venomous mob,
stare at long blonde hair snake down
the thin channel of a teenage girl's back.

Death knots a century of screams
beneath the moon's weeping white eye.

How?

For Breonna Taylor

How long will
Angels of peace have to beat their patient wings hard against this
violent air,
Navigate through this dense forest of
Growing un-
Rest? Rest? How? When anger, that off-key
Yodeler, sings through the limbs of so many night-colored bodies.

Again

Last night's food riots in my stomach
as I watch millions of eyes watch
a black man's life end in the street —
the weight of a knee on his neck
      for eight minutes.
The *Blue* pressing his knee listens,
hands in his pockets, to the bound man
cry out for his mother.
His mother's grave cries.
His brother pleads,
"My family wants peace."

After his lifted knee, did the officer go home
make a peanut butter and jelly sandwich, kiss his wife,
wash guilt from his hands?

Pain, that strong current, rips through the world,
its waves crushing as massive stones.
Descendants, non-descendants of slaves are feathers
on injustice's cruel bird.
Unrest dirties the night with orange flames —
anger rumbles through crowds
mixed with mourners and mutineers.
Why does innocence draw disgrace?
Can spirits rust?
Who can place a curfew on despair?
What saw can slice a wall of indifference?

A trio of *Blues* refuses to serve and protect
another black man.
Their silence — his death.

Why I Stopped Watching the Trial of Derek Chauvin

Because my fingers rolled into boulders
when the defense attorney spoke.

Because my pulse became a padless mallet
pounding my chest,
a warning sign from my heart —
disdain for the defense attorney
is a dangerous disease.

Because my anger became a mountain
after I heard a child's traumatized voice
recite a narrative of death,
after, I heard George Floyd plead,
say, "Please" and "Thank you,"
after Chauvin said, "Uh-huh,"
after the defense attorney spoke
I smashed the air with an ugliness
murderers would applaud.

Because there was no language
my helplessness could speak,
I battered the ironing board
and raged at crooning birds for their happiness.

Because I cried.
Because blame, that venomous poison,
flowed in my veins,
I blamed the breath of those I never met — will meet,
history's broken scales, and the defense attorney's
entourage of experts.

Because hate is a knee on the neck,
bullet in the back,

nasty words in the wounds of the broken,
shame arrested me.

Because
I became
everything I despised.

Remembering Our Roots

History, that ancient tour guide, admonishes —
wear gratitude's shoes when you travel
through the past's dense forest.
In this sacred place, the incense of sacrifice
and slaughter still burns in the trees.
The carcasses of those whose bones were broken
with chains and rods,
flesh carved with whips and blades
and those who witnessed lives savagely torn apart
are buried on these old roads.
Their tears are enough to fill a dried river.

How many times did those mournful souls cry out
to the heavens?
Whose arms are strong enough to lift us from this misery?
Whose countenance is tough enough to battle injustice?
Whose voice is mightier than those who rule with brutality?

A peoples' dignity was ground down to the color of air
so others may justify the cruelties of their hearts.
Back before our forefathers knew the yolk of slavery
another people group cried out to the Lord.
When I read of my forefathers' faith and struggles,
wisdom and strength, it is as if they are calling out to me
in the chattering wind. I want to tell the wind,
the world, with all of its noise, *hush*.

Forget your broken vows — old rejoicings.
The cargo of regret is too heavy to carry
in the deep cavities of your body, and your joys
are history too.
Live in the promise of now.

Change and the unknown are heads on the same coin.
Yes, child, look back at the past, do not linger there;
keep your eyes forward and your voice lifted in praise.
If you keep looking back at lost innocence,
you'll miss the small wings of light
guiding you to a life with liberties
far greater than you can envision.

What Is

1

Dripping with death,
COVID is an umbrella
and one million souls
are evaporated raindrops.

2

Fire is rain in California, Colorado, Washington, Oregon
with air the color of burning.
I know a poet in Oregon who lost her house and farm to flames —
everything made with hands,
stones, and the splintered bodies of trees.
Gladness! Her spirit remains in the flesh,
rooted in the here and now.

3

Hurricane Sally, with her robust appetite,
ties on her September bib,
tries to swallow Alabama whole,
chews at one-hundred five miles per hour —
eight more join the vanished.

4

Black Lives Matter, still, only to some.
A Zoom poetry reading I attend is crashed
by "Jenna Bowser" who writes NIGGERS in chat,
fires obscenities from the cannon of her mouth,
face hidden behind a black screen.

5

Ruth Bader Ginsburg is dead.
Election Day climbs the steep stairs of anticipation
and the governor brews a potion to make ballot boxes
disappear; this hurts my heart

like the sharp axe of tongue chopping at a child's ears
with cruel insults.

5

Is power deadlier than disease?
Is it a disease?
Is disease power?

6

A vote is one flame. One raindrop. One storm.
Change is a hoarse troubadour.
Words are ghosts
flying in and out of our bones.

A Professor Ate an Apple
When She Accused Me of Lying

When I sail in anonymity's yacht,
praise squeezes its lush juices
into my ears.
The day comes when my skin drydocks
inside my name written beneath a poem.

I unveil myself, a tall mocha latte,
to Professor C.
Her brooding eyes peer at me
from over rectangular black-rimmed glasses.
Somewhere in our linage,
we both have an African Queen Mother.

Dignity skips away from her high-yellow face
when she saws through a Gala apple,
masticates its red flesh without pity.
Core and seeds inch toward the roof of her mouth
when she says my words are not my own.

I feel like that butchered apple,
integrity churned down to the core,
when she says, *I love this poem.*
You can't write anything like this.
Black people don't write this way.

I stare as scarlet flecks slothfully drool
from the corners of her cruel lips,
point to my name, *This is me. This is me.*

I tire from pleading my integrity.
After I catch, release my breath like a gentle rain,
silence falls over her insult, my anger.

Two Americas

"The world is always crazy.
The joy of fun is to forget it momentarily."
— Myron Meisel

The sky is a mortuary for stars.
I learn how to murder
watching endless hours
of *Snapped, Forensic Files,*
Vengeance Killings...

Death is interrupted with images
my mind tries to bury.
Prince Policeman dressed in his riot gear escorts
Cinderella down three hundred sixty-five steps
after she leaves the rags of her disdain
inside the capitol.

My body is a glass of disbelief;
I pour myself into bed.
The liquid of my eyes leaks down
my cheeks to my chest
as I watch Prince's counterpart
abandon his promise to protect and serve.
His oath, a broken stem of trust as he poses
alongside one who batters democracy —
their image a memoir of pride.

The flag pops in the breeze
as compassion shoots blanks.
With every push, punch, shattered piece of glass,
some who wear the name of Christ
prove their hate for the created is greater
than their love for *The Creator.*

In the rotunda, capitol walls weep
as they witness Brian D. Sicknick's strength
folded in the corners of *Old Glory*.
Eduardo Nicolas Alvear Gonzalez tweets
his smoke infested joy,
"Glass was broken, offices were barged into…
People got hurt."

Sleep eludes me, I stare into the backyard
where a lone bulb attempts to touch its round shadow.
My mind, a dazed loop, replays the part of the day
where the children sing songs about picking peas
and banana slugs and we laugh and laugh and laugh
until our laughter are tears —
veils to conceal tattered innocence.

The Alphabet of Survival and Sailing
in the Deep Ocean of Pandemic

Over one hundred days we ride harsh waves
of the unknown on an ocean of dis-ease.
Some of us in: auxiliary ships,
barges, catamarans.

Some of us in dhows, electric cruisers, ferries,
gondolas, hovercrafts, amphibious beings
skirting one another's breaths.

Some of us in ice, junks, kayaks, liners,
missile cutters, unwilling weapons
aimed at the innocent and vulnerable.

Some of us in Norlands, optimists, on pontoons,
Q-ships, rafts, primitive propellers of arms
shoving through fear's deep waters.

Some of us in skiffs, tankers, umiaks,
slender vessels, wave-piercing crafts
stabbing through the rough sea of indifference.

Some of us in wherries, xebecs, yachts,
Zillen — stable, secure from tipping
into lack or want.

Some of us on dollar store floaties,
in punctured life jackets, raggedy garments,
naked, bodiless.

Who among us can survive a damaged hull?
Who among us take their eyes off the bow?
Who among us loved ones is counted
on a death toll clicker?

A Letter to the Vaccine

I will not strap miracle across your back,
burden you with such a task, title.
I am twice grateful for the prick and sting
that sent you like a current in the river
of my blood.
I allowed you to swim inside my veins
because I want to do more than walk
on the crunchy sentences of dried fallen leaves
and listen to the erratic rhythms of bird feathers
flapping in the branches of trees.
How grateful I am to walk among air and light.
But I want to return
to the Jack-in-the Box kids at the movies,
the ones who pop up and down in their seats
to go get popcorn, nachos, napkins, to the bathroom.
I even want the ones who hold a one-sided conversation
with characters on the screen.
Give me the mother who shushes them
with a volume louder than their monologues.
Her shushing an aria I didn't know to applaud.
I want to return to the gymnasium,
listen to the beat and bounce of a basketball
on hardwood, the spectators' cheers, the blink
of the scoreboard, and the loud buzzer
signaling time has run out.
I want to return to a time when it was safe
to inhale/exhale as a lovesick newlywed thrust
a Bath & Body Works fragrance at my nose
and asked "Do you think she will like it?"
Then walked away as if my smile and his choice
formed an allegiance.

Vaccine, I entered in a union with you
because I would like to sit freely in this earth,
skin to sky, and watch clouds embellish the horizon.

Will We Desire Touch?

After the COVID-19 kryptonite
is discovered, will we desire touch —
that primitive longing
swaddled in our lives before birth?
Will it be more desirable
than clasping light between our teeth
in a world darkening with dread?

Before this phantom smuggled
panic into our lives,
beliefs broke friendships,
family relationships,
kind words became crushed bricks,
crumbled from the weight
of anger's battering.

Curious how this fear forces wide
        the circle of distance,
how the invisible separates us.

And those souls who depend on a stranger's touch
for comfort: a brush of fingertips from the grocery clerk,
a bump from the waitress burdened with too many trays,
a pat on the back from the worker at a soup kitchen,
the volunteer who rocks an orphaned child
in the neonatal intensive-care unit.
Is there a surrogate for the warm arch of flesh?

Oh! To fill air and lungs, lives and loneliness
with the dust of crushed kind words.
Let their film cover computer,
telephone, television screens.

Let their residue stick to hands flush against glass
as they reach for companionship from the pit of isolation.
And for those whose hands cannot reach
beyond cardboard boxes, may they hear
friendly voices echoing from heart-to-heart
in this dark season of distancing.

Part 4: Rehabilitation

Epistle 4:

Late one Friday night, I was visiting with my friend, Sue, via phone when she said, "Lo, I think I am depressed." I responded, "Sue half the world is depressed. We have been isolated for eight months."

I entered into the pandemic season carrying depression in the luggage of my mind, a third diagnosis of cancer and the loss of friends and loved ones, in addition to other issues. Also, I was also carrying the challenging stories and secrets of others inside of me. This space honors those mental issues pre-COVID and during COVID.

The wound is the place where the light enters.
— Rumi

I Am a Falling Sky

I watch a fat white moon hatch
from an egg of darkness.
Wonder if the air will peel
the blackness from my body
when I scrape against its invisible wall.
I hear the surprised grass
after softly landing on wild fields
of bluebonnets.

A band of fire ants marches
beneath the heavy beat of a spring sun
in their red uniforms
as the wind plays slow cadences.
How far must they go
before winter locks them
below ground with its cold hands?

I want to see the day grow taller,
watch spidery arms of light web
a clump of weeds struggling through
a pile of stones in the back flower garden.

I pretend the horizon is a soft pair of hands
like the ones my foremothers had before
picking cotton, before digging into cotton sheets
as cruelty was thrust into their bodies,
and foul words tried to abolish the ghosts
of their innocence.

I cry at the desperate chirping of a lost baby sparrow,
its injured wing too fragile to lift it from fear.
Maybe my sorrow is for all lost and fallen things,

the marginalized, the troughs of hate filled with blood,
an earth big with beauty and ugliness.
I feel 7.5 billion bodies
swelling with a desire for kindness.
I can carry a country in my mouth.
Where shall I take it?
I worry I will swallow the wrong flag.
Maybe it's because I am a falling sky.
I understand the exchange between sun and moon
each day after holding up the weight of their light.
Even they know the mind needs rest
from too much affliction and jubilation.
Balance is glue, and I try not to hold
onto what I cannot change or undo,
Dream an ocean of forgiveness.
When I close my eyes, I am neither ocean nor a black
woman, teacher, painter, poet — only a sky
falling into a white so translucent there is nothing.

Rehabilitation

Too many years she tries to eat wishes,
gobble up morsels her mind warns to avoid.
She buys him another plaid shirt he will not wear,
gives him a birthday card he can't read,
wait for acknowledgement that will never come.

One week into rehab the therapist instructs her
to love, affirm, support herself. How?
She tells everything wrong with herself instead.
The therapist's question is a mantra,
"Can't you find something positive to say?"
She can't.
Her daddy's rejection is a leech,
sucks her into insanity,
leaves her mind like tonight's storm.

Black cowls of clouds obstruct the stars,
long fangs of lightning bite across the sky.
When thunder finally explodes
into shards of silence, she walks onto the patio,
finds a dried withered leaf
tucked safely beneath the awning.
When she picks it up,
that leaf crumbles underneath the weight
of her inspection.
She will crumble like this, too,
she tells the therapist in the next session.

"Write him a letter; tell everything
you want him to know, "the therapist says.
"He can't read," she tells her.
"The letter is not for him; it's for you,"
therapist says.

"Why do I need to write what I already know?"
she asks.

Therapist points to the blank pages
of her notebook,
"If you write, there will be no need to purge."
She looks at therapist,
expression distant as the stars.

Six weeks into rehab, the insurance company
writes her a letter, informs you have two days
left of rehabilitation.
The therapist writes a prescription,
"These will help you focus."

She drives away with bulimia
scribbling on her throat,
listing every wish it will not give her.

Shades of Hope

The cupboard of myself esteem is empty —
no bones, no bread, no Daddy.
He is a bountiful meal of preoccupation.

I take depression as a lover.
He cloaks himself in hunger.
All day I give him lavish gifts of food,
Binge and purge to please him.
In return, he gives me shame as a wedding band,
keeps me yoked to his "Daddy obsession."

Standing on the edge of humiliation,
I curse the smug porcelain bowl
that has become the center of my life.
With its mouth wide open, spittle clear and still,
it dares me to empty myself into it once more.
Postured to release my lover's gifts
into that deep cavity of lust,
I turn instead, rail in the mirror.
Wail at the person I did not want to be.

At work, a student stands in a chair screaming
for attention.
This is the only way he knows to say I trust you.

I retaliate, scream at him, my face flared with fury.
He stares at me, eyes emptied of joy.
I check myself into *Shades of Hope*.
This is the only way I know to say I am sorry.

Waiting with a Stranger

He rivals Michelangelo's David
with his chiseled face, muscular physique,
boulder-hard biceps tattooed with a cross
and other symbols I can't decipher.
We stand outside a door where laughter bangs
hard against the wood.
Our bodies too far for touch,
near enough to hear heavy inhales, exhales.
A Coach bag hangs from my shoulder,
a pink Hello Kitty from his.
His palms paddle in his pants pockets
as he shifts his weight with impatience.
We exchange glances in a sudden halo of silence.
 A burst of noise. The door flings open,
a high-pitched voice screams *Daaadd-dy!*
I stare when he swoops up
his cherub-nosed daughter.
Her response, a confirmation of ritual.
Thin arms clutch his thick neck.
Wheat-colored curls drape his left ear.
Small fingers fidget in the gully
of his wide back.
He christens her forehead with a quick peck.

A memory presses against my heart.
I am ten. June's blooming with heat.
My daddy, his new wife cruise beside me
with the smell of new leather wafting
through a partially lowered window.
With a faux smile she asks,
"So, what did you get Robert for Father's Day?"
With body slouched, head dropped

like a drooping zinnia, I tell her, "Nothing"
as I reach for the back-door handle.
They drive away, wave,
leave me standing on the sidewalk
soaked in a well of shame.
Streams of laughing voices drench my memories.
Like a wet puppy, I shake the past until my mind
returns to the cheerful hallway where I waited
with a stranger I now dub Father of the Year.
When he walks away with his daughter,
the little girl inside of me cries,
Don't Leave. Please don't leave me!

Talking to Fear

after Denise Levertov, Talking to Grief

*The Wawel Dragon is a fabled mythological
dragon in Polish folklore*

Fear, you are as the Wawel Dragon,
an oppressive reptile living
in the cave of my stomach;
your large bones crush against my ribs.
I don't want you.

If I hunt you,
wrestle you in your own lair,
pin you down,
stuff your fiery mouth with snow,
will this end you?

You think I don't know you want my peace
as an offering of appeasement.
You think I don't know your real desire
is the tender maiden of my heart. You need
its innocence.
You need the way it freely opens
like a lost lamb,
easily devoured.
But it knows pain.
Pain is the greater fire.
You are
a dwindling kindle.

The Power of Guilt

Cristobal Rojas, Venezuela, 1890, El Purgatorio

The fire of Rojas' guilt
coaxed Sun out of the sky.
For flame calls unto flame.
Day descended into night.
Time died.
The sun became an ambient orange light,
an agony of darkness.
Rojas' conscience, red
as blood, fear, regret
hovered over an altar of hands
made from souls he never touched.

The First Time I Taste Wine from Your Lips

After the seasons make their rounds,
the air in my overcrowded hometown smells of crude oil
and an economy-sized can of Glade floral room freshener.

Spring with its history of fussy barometric pressures
is on rotation when I lick the last of the Pinot Noir?
Zinfandel? Merlot? from the rim of your mouth.
Before you, I only knew Thunderbird
from a dare. Sixteen, trying to prove I was more woman
than girl.

Now that I taste a full glass of you,
the flavor of red fermented grape skins
rushes like a torrent of water
through every place in the building of my body.

Three intense years we drink each other's passion,
desire pulses in our fingertips when we touch.
We can make the characters in *Fifty Shades of Gray* blush.

How could I have known next year at this time
my shoulders would ache with sadness, my heart
would break like a fragile rope?

How could I have known you would brush my hand
away when I reached for you, my tears would be as rust
on the spiny scales of your resistance?

How do I cleanse my palate of you,
discipline my tongue to appreciate
the taste of someone else's words?
Time.

Mending is an unending business;
this earth is filled with broken hearts in need of repair —
including yours.

Three times I ask you to stay.
Three times you go back to her.
Three years later you say,
I made a mistake. Let's renew what we had.
Darling, you cannot pour new wine in old wineskins.
Do you expect me to spill the new strength of my heart
on our ruined past?
In a ritual of spring cleaning,
I crank up Cool & the Gang,
lip-synch *Celebration*.
After I finish the closets, I start on the dressers.
The day you left, you left your fraternity jacket,
I found it buried in the bottom of a drawer, aging.

Why I Can't Keep a Lover

After I tell you innocence is not ripped out,
rather rammed into the psyche,

your eyes are like last night's hard rain.
Sometimes the story is the breaking

up.
I woke this morning

with my fingernails digging into my arm.
I dreamt you were falling

into the deep cavern of dark clouds.
You reached for me.

I was not trying to pull you out.
I was trying to thrust you deeper

into the darkness,
further away from the truth

of my broken skin.

While Standing in Line to Pay for My Groceries, I Play Angry Birds Video Game on My Phone

I do not ask why
these wingless birds are yellow with anger,
white with fury, red with contempt
and black with such malice
they allow themselves to be propelled
against stone and wood walls time and time
and again, to bring down the temple
on the heads of green pigs.

How far back does this feud go?

An ally of the fowls,
I do not ask what treason
these sows committed.
My obedient clueless
fingers become a slingshot,
launch some other animal's anger
into the glassy ether of my phone.

I convince myself this bloodless
violent lust is harmless.
Until I do not destroy the sows' dreams.
Until I do not reach the next level.
Until grunts break from my bones.

Until I see a wide-eyed child in a shopping basket
tracing me with her fear,
the wings of my angry breath flap rapidly
through the long line.

How must I have looked to her?
Head bowed, face contorted, hand frantic
with anger.

Easter is a calendar page away.
The department store's decals of happy
pink and blue chicks pecking at the windows

make me smile after I turn away from my game.
Is this the way to banish anger —
to turn away from…?
In my purse, the slinging continues.
There is no white flag, not even for Jesus.

A Love Letter to the Part of My Body I Despise

My friend says, "You have a big butt."
I pull my blouse down to veil you —
an inheritance from my ancestors.

I ask her, "What are you doing looking?"
She says, "I am jealous. I want one.
You have the hips to go with it."

I am sorry her words are a net
over my self-consciousness—
her opinion lord over my body.

Do you remember when I was younger?
Men thought their lust made me deaf.
"Man! Look at that butt! Umm…"

I blamed you for their desire.
Despised your full firm roundness.
Desperately tried to wish you away.

Why is it the blackbirds know
you my booty, my bottom, my bum
should be celebrated?

From tree branches, they make leaves shake
like pom-poms, honor your power,
the way you move against gravity.

On this turquoise-colored day,
you are a lioness, seraph, goddess —
worshiped with their black wings spread wide,
their flight a chorus of hallelujahs.

Oh, the birds, how they embrace the air!
The flight of their meaning is for me to track them
to the breast of sky blushed with a cloud named Kindness.

Oh, butt! I will not ask her to kiss you.
I will not let my voice rage like wildfires
against the mention or your bigness.

I will invite her to sit down, marvel at the images
sprawled across the heavens — a pair of opened arms
to welcome those bruised by words.

Symphony of Snow

The Valentine's Day before this one,
before the world spurned and masked itself,
before pain was the only diagnosis in my back,
before cancer crashed through the window, again,
before the clots in my lungs,
before my mind was filled with embers of panic,
before the long empty corridors of the hospital,
before my sister had to change my bloody bandages,
before my four-year-old nephew woke me singing
the McDonald's jingle, "I'm Loving It,"
before he helped his mother record the fluid
pumped from my breast,
before my world tumbled into a field of fear,
I was in San Antonio where The Mariachi's brass
and string melodies floated across the Riverwalk.
At Panchito's Mexican Restaurant, puffy tacos
made my palate laugh.

This Valentine's Day
the compositions of streets and horizon
are in the same sharp white key.
Listen to this symphony of wind and snow,
the hiss of bushes, the creak and crunch
of leather on ice, the crack of wood, squoosh of melt.
Tonight, after callous snow, wild winds,
and breath crippling cold temperatures
return to their beginning,
an entourage of stars treks across the translucent sky.
In the shadows, leafless branches
and the high wooden fence press their faces
against the window's naked pane.
I draw the curtains to keep them out.

Perhaps they remind me
of a faceless figure in my dreams.
Perhaps it's because I am full from lugging
other people's secrets in my body.

Part Five: Ways of Coping during COVID

Epistle 5:

Like millions of others, I searched for various ways to cope during this COVID season. Much of it is spent taking trips to the oncology center for treatment. Before returning to the classroom, I spent time binge watching television, assembling jigsaw puzzles, reading, writing, taking virtual museum trips, participating/ presenting in Zoom readings, watching YouTube videos, and attending online workshops, and taking walks when possible.

My greatest challenges and greatest rewards manifested by returning to the classroom face-to-face. My oncologist released me to work with the stipulations I wear a mask, face shield, and adhere to social distancing. This created another level of isolation because I spent the majority of the school term eating lunch alone. Fortunately, I have a young assistance I could visit with from across the room.

Besides teaching music, some of my other responsibilities include, outside morning duty and cafeteria duty. My scheduled shift is with the younger students, kindergarten through third grades. What a chore to keep the students socially distanced. Six feet of distancing is a wall they are determined to climb. They want to touch, talk, more than they want to eat. It hurts my heart every time I tell one to turn around, eat, return to your seat. I worry about the long-term effect COVID will have on their mental wellbeing. My greatest joy comes on those days when they can go outside, scream, run, play, and be children. When possible, I walk to the playground so I can hear their laughter.

The world masked herself.
Somehow we learned to unveil hate.
Somehow we learned to unveil love.
Somehow we learned to unveil ourselves.

When My Sister Said, "Put on Your Shoes," My Nephew Asked, "Is COVID Over?"

How do you explain to a five-year-old
life is an organism continually mutating
and the earth still cannot breathe?

How do you elucidate time is a weathered barrel
and providence is the sailor who will guide us
across the waters of un-normalcy?

How do you plainly say anxiety is a stringent vine
threading through the psyche
and those maskless day are gifts
we were too busy to write thank you notes for?

When the air dances
in a ballroom filled with waltzers
and risk is no longer the color of iron,

I will politely bump into a stranger,
look her in the eyes as I sketch her
into my memory.
I will say excuse me,
but not apologize.

The Bengal Tiger canna lilies growing
in my garden know only the sky's
golden veil can conceal the breadth
of longing in my eyes,
to again be vulnerable.
To again
have my face
naked.

What Kindergartners Taught Me about COVID During Cafeteria Duty

Children carry the sun in their hearts.
Their desire and need for each other are atoms
fusing into exuberant chortles.
The gravity of touch is an immense draw.
They stretch their bodies across cafeteria stools.
Their hands are rays reaching for each other.
Skin-upon-skin is a flame when their fingers touch —
their smiles torches of intimacy.
Why must I extinguish this fire of longing?
Isn't this a reason we create boundaries?
To shrink the world into a caged entity?
They sit erect until I transition to another table.

My words are a cloud of dust.
The sun does not understand darkness.
How can I break this cycle of constant reaching
when my desire is to orbit around their light?

After Strolling Across the Playground, I Stand at the End of "B" Wing and Watch Students Leave for Home

Little Hansels and Gretels funnel out through
yellow steel doors of an elementary schoolhouse
into the disease-riddled forest of uncertainty.

They are clueless
to the crumbs of their youthful forgetfulness.
Sprinkled across the playground, a trail of masks:
one under an oak older than this 1950's building,
one near the jungle gym, one near the sandpit,
and in the air, expectations
of these little ones to remain safe.

A gentle breeze delivers a Spider Man mask
six feet away from where I stand.
It catches on the corner of a concrete slab —
an impotent hero.

Longing, not sadness,
is the cartilage in the bones of my thoughts.
Such desire for those days before COVID.
Such desire to live beyond COVID.
Such desire for the resurrection of fearless touch.

I cover my face, walk inside,
leave the scent of a child's breath
caught in Spider Man's tiny black web.

Ode to Cracker Jacks

Giddy as a child, I tear the cellophane wrapper's grip
from the *Things I Ate as a Kid* 1,000-piece puzzle box.
I read the name of each snack, drink, boxed meal, smile
at the ones I can still get from a grocery shelf.
A hodgepodge of flavors competes for a space on the cover —
the salty crunch of Fritos, sweet cold of Popsicles,
carbonated fizz of Bubble Up.
A blizzard of colorful cardboard falls
as I pour pieces onto tagboard,
each shape different as fingerprints.

I sift through the pile in search of edges,
cluster like colors, find an eye among the pinks,
mustache in the blues, "nose" among the whites.
Isn't this the way we shape our being, framing edges,
clustering, sifting through partial pieces to make a whole?
Isn't this the beauty of time, to connect each vine of thought,
plan, dream as we watch our lives form?

My hands carry me back to that happy place
where I climbed trees, played with tea sets, made mud pies
as I lock matching pieces together, rejoice when
Cracker Jacks, Wonder Bread, CHEEZ-IT,
Fiddle Faddle, Captain Crunch, Kool-Aid are complete.
A flame of need for a moment in my past burns in me —
age ten, I run up and down Carver Street screaming with laughter
until the sky drains itself of blue.
The past is a wet wick I cannot ignite.
I walk to the pantry get a bag of CHEEZ-IT —
my tongue cannot tell the difference between then and now.

Watching an Episode of Hoarders

Joanna Robertson revealed in 2016, a relative
of blind hoarder Rita Wolfensohn went upstairs
and found the skeleton of Rita's son, still in the
clothes he died in. He'd been dead for 20 years.

Rita doesn't have the heart to let go
of things.
Perhaps this is the reason her house is a landfill
of clutter and filth.
Did she sleep with the naked one-armed doll
on the apex of this mountain of debris
when she was a child?
Dream this rusty tireless tricycle its chariot?
Did she hear rats ripping through the headlines
of twenty-year-old newspapers?
Did she wear this dirty red polka-dot dress,
battered white pumps, broken headband
on her first date?

How can she eat from this congested kitchen
spoiled with gallons of milk, withered lettuce,
thawed frozen pizzas, bags of onions…?
Not smell the stench of food and waste
putrefaction — enough to mask death?
What strong grief wrestles her into obsession?
The second floor, a burial ground of excess,
is her son's dirty tomb.
For two decades, darkness held a vigil for him —
waiting for someone to change his grave clothes.
Waiting for someone to give his bones to the earth.

Her body convulses with fear,
fingers are like pliers when asked to part with:
a jungle of plastic plants, dumpsters of dog food,

a battalion of empty beverage bottles,
hundreds upon hundreds of stuffed animals —
other possessions too mammoth to record.
Is this how death can live in the house of a body?
The mind becomes cocooned in traps of the past?

Oh, Rita, what did your heart lose?
What does it want?
What sadness is hidden in these treasures
you cannot press against your bosom?
Is it because you lost the music of your eyes?

With Regards to T.O., I Mix My Metaphors

Sunday, game day. I watch
helmets collide, players hauled away
on stretchers, referees stretching their arms
heavenward, proclaiming some sort of goodness.
In judgement, I cock my tongue
with unflattering expletives, fire at Terrell's
loud grandstanding and harsh words
aimed at his teammates.

Time, the tatty luggage of our minds,
carries change in its ageless handles.
Now I watch Terrell on *Iyanla Fix My Life* —
not the pigskin running man
with dollars dwindling in his pockets.
The eleven-year-old with truth's smoke
pluming through cracks where stern punishment,
withheld affection, and deceit broke his heart.
A tidal wave of tears crashes against his woeful face
after Iyanla exhumes his graved pain.
How is he to relearn the language of innocence
after learning the neighbor's eyes across the street
are those of his father?

My apologies Terrell.
Now I understand the ecosystem of your life,
learn these lessons: the sky has no clock
yet it knows when to spin its color-wheel.
If, that conditional banner, constantly flaps
overhead.
Bro/ken requires new words —
           restoration/healing
are long-distance runners.

Do not hesitate — run
towards the wild animal of joy.
If you suddenly feel the pulse of its heart
in your hand, do not let go.

In Search of a Father

After viewing Detail of Child's Play 69, Tom Jackson

It is dangerous to confront the heart
with what you won't do.
It will challenge you to a game of chicken.

Even when your body is stacked with decades,
it will reduce you to a child.
Will send you pecking through a flock of people
at a theater in search of a father.

You will flatten your eight-year-old self,
become a shadow,
back against chairs
as you inch past two jovial ladies.
The way their wide smiles swallow joy whole
stall you.
You pause in front of the lady with the pillbox hat,
her energetic countenance a welcome mat.
Even the scar on her left cheek looks like laughter.

Your heart will whisk your eyes
away from the lady behind her.
The one whose glasses rest on the bridge of her sadness,
sight focused on the door.
Her expression looks like hope spun backwards.
Perhaps she is waiting for someone
she hopes she has not lost.

It will make you look at the man behind you.
The chic one with a crisp collar, rakish chin and nose.
Smooth cleft lips sealed like a kissed envelope.
Hair the color of ravens' wings.
Tadpole shaped brows etched on his forehead.

Choose him.
He will lift you from the shadows,
feed you more goodness than the man
who spilled his seeds, left you in this world
scratching dirt like a chicken for his affection.

Rereading the Biography of Harriet Tubman

February, teacher unveils Harriet's history,
school children rehearse the narrative of her bravery.
The way she smuggles night-skinned families
away from those who rule
with whips and chains, dogs and disdain,
guns and gruff inhumanity.
How can they convince themselves
their cruelty is ordained by God,
her supposed duty is to welcome
lashes and insults with gratitude?
Such a beast, slavery.
Centuries of rain cannot rinse away
stolen blood nor can generations
of prayers repair families broken by servitude.

What courage to travel night's dense wooded roads,
depend on maps of stars, kindness of strangers,
bed in graveyards.
The moon should tell her stories,
a daughter who refuses bondage,
a broken-hearted woman who will not be broken,
a warrior for women.

I fall asleep with the biography of her life
open on my chest.
I cannot stop dreaming her spirit,
wake with the crust of her power flaked over my body.

Outside robins sing their same ancient birdsong,
I imagine her silhouette carved on driftwood
floating on the tide of morning.

Four Thursdays before Christmas,
I Talk to Three Five-Year-Olds

"Tomorrow is God's birthday,"
a kindergartener informs me.
"Today is Taco Tuesday,"
another chimes in.
From the dark sky of my sweater,
Rudolph's moon-shaped nose swells
above a blood-colored banner
stenciled with *Santa Loves Me!*
The third child snickers and points,
"Santa loves you. Santa loves you.
It's right there on your sweater. See?"
I look down at the banner and see
love has been before me all morning.
Isn't wisdom ethereal in the mouth of children?
Isn't it lovely time is a threadless needle
in the fabric of their lives?
One can have God, tacos, and love in any season.

The trio seizes my heart with merry words.
When it is returned, gift-wrapped
in bright ribbons of their innocence, I laugh.

How I wish I could give such merriment.
How I wish I could make my spirit a star.
How I wish I could give an eight-year-old
legs like Fred Astaire after he reveals,
"My Christmas wish is to learn how to dance."

Part Six: Witnessing the Seasons Pass

Epistle 6:

Relentless, seasons return and depart with joy, uncertainty, trauma, hope in their bottomless trunks. Three hundred sixty-five days they make the same endless loop, land in the same spot on the real estate of calendar. They move through the familiar station of sequence: winter, spring, summer, fall. For me, there is comfort in the predictability of calendar days and beauty in the unpredictability and diversity of the seasons, the surprises they gift each day.

I wasn't aware that words could hold so much.
I didn't know a sentence could be so full.
— Delia Owens, "Where the Crawdads Sing"

I Want to Dream of Peacocks and Ducks

Memories of my dreams, rare like Tanzanite.
Three vivid as the violet stone.

Hurricane
a tree yanked up by the trunk
roots sprawled like a web of chaos
a perfect round chasm left
deep in the universe
my voice the color of darkness

Arch
an archway of doors
light calls to me like a song
I follow its melody
my body pirouettes toward
every beautiful thing
that filled the trunk of my existence
I cannot carry

Faceless
a baby in an incubator
soft on its stomach
its form a silhouette of mystery
small hands clinched closed
breath odorless

I tap the glass
it does not stir
perhaps this is the way silence cries

I draw a crescent moon in my hand,
chew my bottom lip as my nails sink
into the frail cradle.

I Have Been Miss February for Sixty Years

I pad my body with a heavy over-sized coat,
long beige scarf, forget my gloves,
head into Thursday.

I walk through the *Dollar Store* with my crown
of black kinky hair streaked with gray.
I feel extra eyes follow my gift-wrapped
night-colored skin.

I am the eyes of the eighty-six-year-old
white-haired lady who can't find what she needs.
Stealthily she approaches from behind,
touches my arm, startles me.
Her frame looks as if she weighs the same
as her age, skin pastier than Snow White.
She picks up her three-toed cane,
grabs my arm for support,
"Honey can you show me the light-bulbs?"

"Sure," I say, walk away, a sleuth in search
of one hundred watts, leave her near a shelf
lined with Tide, Downy and Gain.
I find a clerk, rehearse my needs,
the two of us stoop, rummage
through a small assortment of brands —
Philips, GE, Westinghouse.

A feathery touch, then heat grazes my shoulder.
Startled, I turn, find my new friend standing
behind me.
I lift-up a Sylvania 4-pack, ask if this will do.
She nods in the affirmative.
When I stretch myself to full height,

her left hand holds my right arm hostage.
We walk down the crowded aisle
together, our bodies the color of a panda,
towards the register.
When she rummages through her purse then palms
a wad of money, my body cringes with fear.

"I will pay for yours, too, since you helped me,"
she tells me.
"No," I say too forcefully.
My voice mocks the fear I try to hide.
She waits until I am finished with my transaction,
reaches for my arm again.
"Your mother is proud of you," she tells me.
"My mother is dead," I do not say.
We amble out as the sky scolds the city
with vicious cold.
I hover around the door — the watched
now the watcher, wait for her to drive away.

My eyes track the exhaust from her pipes
until she is out of the parking lot.
Until I feel the slack in the leash of suspicion
the clerk hooked on my neck
the moment she saw my crown.

This is not Vincent van Gogh's' Starry Night

The Starry Night
Vincent van Gogh, 1889

In this normally loud month of March,
I stand on the front porch,
lean into this night drenched with quiet,
lift my head wonder if stars dream their light,
speak the same dialect as my eyes?

In the middle of my yard, an old massive mulberry.
Unlike Vincent's flaming cypress, it does not connect
earth and sky in the noisy hamlet of my mind.
I squint my eyes at the mulberry's labyrinth
of naked branches, ask a twisted skinny branch
if the line between madness and sorrow
is made of silk?

I tell myself, You are not Van Gogh
and this is not his night sky
with its rolling energy and exploding stars.
That large white ball at the tip of your tree is not Venus.
It is the moon draped in a shawl of clouds.
His sweeping pale swirls are not the constellation
of cancer cells you saw on your right breast x-ray.
Van Gogh is gone. Your breast is gone. You are here.

If you must walk your life into a painting,
live in Vincent's incessant waves of blue
where those yellow stars are the faces of angels

you can only see in darkness.

Poetry Is

Poetry is the soul's microscope.
That powerful eye that sees beyond
what is beneath the hidden.
It is society's archivist.
The record keeper of all deeds
gardened beneath the sun.
It is a coin minted in questions and answers,
God's seventh right hand,
the simplicity and complexity of
what is.

Rainwater for Geraniums

Dripping with both healing and affliction
I paddle through the nation of my body
seeking refuge from pandemic fatigue —
that all-consuming wall I reduce to a trellis
in my garden.

My face naked with heat,
I exhume weeds, root sweet potato vines
between the rose bushes' stone skirts,
leave the geraniums in a blue porcelain pot.

Memorial Day, flags flap presto as the wind
rushes its tempo and rain wafts through streets.
The meditative tinkle of windchimes shifts
to erratic rattles, thunder's bass drum booms.
Lightning blitzes electric lines— a blink,
the house is drenched in silence
and a twilight shade of darkness.
The aged spring sky draws bathwater for dusty Odessa.
With torrential jubilation, drops plunge onto the city,
though my ruby-headed geraniums are not thirsty yet.

Anointed with an idea,
I retrieve a two-gallon cooking pot,
inch it past my carport
as rain morphs apocalyptic.
The roof lip, a waterfall.

A new Monday,
I shovel mud-colored rainwater from the stainless-steel pot,
soak the soil where my geraniums bloom,
pour the remaining water diluted with dirt

on the sweet potato vines.
In the kitchen's dry light,
I fill the pot with liquid soap, watch suds rise
like hundreds of tiny pale full moons,
swirl paper towels in the bottom, empty it.
Stubborn sandy grains captured
with last Monday's rain stick to the sides.
Again, and again, I inspect
my fingernails, searching for veiled grains.
I refill the pot, unroll more paper towels, swirl, empty.
I press my hand against the sides the way the preacher did
my face when I was six, when he baptized me
to purify my soul.
I repeat the ritual of filling, swirling, emptying
until my right arm tires.
Until my hand wrinkles.
Until I am sure my mouth will not hold
memories of Monday's dirty rain.

Today the Sun Is a No Show

Flemish artist Simon Denis is best regarded
as an early practitioner of plein-air painting.

June, someone forged Odessa's signature in the air.
This time of year, it mimics the face of a naked furnace,
reeks of sour crude — the smell of money.

This muggy morning,
no trace of the sun's corn-colored cranium.
Did dawn forget to set an alarm?
Maybe sun is stuck in New Zealand
and incapable to call-in from across horizons.

Evening sits on a bench, still waiting.
Sable clouds conspire to conceal its absence,
fail to imitate Simon Alexandre Clément Denis'
Study of Clouds with a Sunset Near Rome,
after rain assails aging azaleas, the city.

A peasant village of sweet potato vines cowers
in red soaked sand as bully rain continues
its ruthless rampage into the night.
Three pink rosebushes form an austere allegiance,
contest rain's slashing with hundreds of thorny fingers.

Three a.m., rain whimpers, morphs into a teary toddler
as wet air and darkness cradle the cotton-colored moon.

Butterfly Music in Two Parts

I

Who will debate a poem is not made of bones?
The soft tissue of its crimson and apricot-
colored marrow is stuffed with creation.
The vertebrate of my spine is thirty-three lines of free verse
only doctors and technicians will read
after a tumor fractures it like an incomplete sentence.

The stanza of hope I deleted yesterday is not gone.
There is no mausoleum for the past.
It reincarnates itself in the taste of Gala apples,
in the circumference of a cow's eyes,
the smell of honeysuckle smeared on a June morning,
a warm damp towel draped over a throbbing back.

Mrs. Forsyth's second grade class tells me
in the center of summer, the sun gets hot.
I say this desert sky is a warehouse of heat,
rain's month-long sabbatical is avaricious,
time with its liquid fingers flows backwards,
and I am more than a cancer diagnosis.

II

I am butterfly music.
A six-year-old singing *Jesus loves the little
children, all the children of the world
red and yellow, black and white...*
in the St. James Baptist Church children's choir
where heat, sweat, and black faces pray for change.

I am a teenager perfumed in hormones,
garbed in homemade leopard-print bellbottoms

at a James Brown concert.
Mr. Brown gyrates across the stage
crooning about *A Man's World, Sex Machine, Cold Sweat*,
I pray the boy two rows up notice the animal of myself.

I am eighteen sandwiched between my mother and aunt
at a BB King concert. Cigarette smoke and liquor odor
are heavy drapes in the ballroom.
Men who could have fathered me toss their eyes
in my direction. I feel the fist of mama's fury
as she jabs at them with a lioness stare.

I hum, sway to *The Thrill is Gone, Rock Me Baby,*
Let the Good Times Roll. The clock rolls time
past two a.m. Bodies stream out into a summer's
early morning where heat doesn't know how to tell time.
Now, Mama and Auntie sleep among the stars.
Each day my body plays a cadenza of healing.

The Window

After viewing Dream III: Who's in the Garden?
Watercolor, ink and collage, Margaret Burnett

Cancer fleeces me for a third time.
Presses fear's muzzle against my chest.
Words huddle behind the door of my throat.

While at the oncology center,
gentlemen avoid my eyes, turn heads
toward the frontier of a clear window.

I pull my T-shirt down past the "V"
of its neck, expose the top portion
of my breast and dark surgical scar —

the gateway to access my new port.
After a savage prick, I nuzzle
my head against the chair's soft leather,

press my hand to water-colored glass,
guiltlessly leave smudges as I reach
for the center's mini-Garden of Eden.

A plant with elephant ears bends down
as a red-headed geranium whispers,
I think one of them has a crush on us —

the one whose hand is on the window.
Her eyes roamed the garden then returned
to our pot. I think she wants to climb inside.

She wants to crush your petals against her face.
Dream the redness in her eyes is not from tears —
they are flowers blooming red.

One Summer Night

August paces as if on a forgotten mission.
The desert sun sweats excess heat.
Days are vast vessels brimmed with scorched air.
Russet patches of grass that pepper narrow streets
are the desert's dossier of weeks with no rain.
Tonight, the wind offers a brief recess.
Stars tussle with stray clouds for a station in the sky.
The sudden hiss and spin of a water sprinkler interrupts
an expressionless darkness, frightens an intruder
in my backyard — a stray calico. It leaps across
the high wooden pickets, its tail fussing with the air.

Fear, my fear, is a passenger in its glassy eyes.
My hand shakes as I toss slices of old bread in the trash.
I can feel my future pass through my throat,
press against my ribs, as I watch the trespasser escape.
Such power in suddenness — the way it grasps breath,
tangles your body in a mass of confusion.

Morning, a stream of brass-colored leaves lines dry streets —
longing for a kiss from the dewless dawn.

Desiccation

Autumn begins by eating dry heat.
Dying in the small backyard, green
clumps of summer.
A slender-legged patio lamp sits on stone pavers,
its silver metal shade an umbrella
for a constant mist of light.
Aging leaves dream of a sparrow's last song.
Near the wooden gate, spider plants crawl over
a planter elevated above the perishing garden —
its plantlets like Lady Liberty's torch. Dusk,
freedom's flames burn in this West Texas sun's
tired red-rimmed eye.

On Posing with Swans

For Lisa Toth Salinas and Courtney O'Banion Smith

We sit beneath a metal sky,
my new friend and I.
Behind us, two swans snub our webless
existence, preen in a faux pond.
Our smiles beam like headlights.
Imitation, quiet as a rainless sky,
creeps into my right arm.
It rests on a partition of glass,
arched like the neck of one of the swans,
hand opened, shaped like its peering
watery black eye.
Across the room, water drips from somewhere.
Curious how fallen things mimic the other —
the swan's white neck, my black arm,
both our tears the color of silence.

Perhaps This Is the Way *It* Happened

Unguarded words slip from Eve's tongue
like stray particles — *I want it.*
They drift through the heavy air,
become breaches in a continuum of story.
A narrative whose origins begin in the womb of time,
before light and darkness were separated.
Is this why day begins when darkness is in full bloom?

Eve bites an apple, crumbles Eden's lavish walls.
This is the power of a woman's words, desire —
to destroy or heal.
This is the power of her body —
to carry change like an unborn child.

Oh, the many faces of want — fruit, serpent, man...
A chameleon lives in infinity's house.
This evening it's a swan drawn on a canvas of clouds.
Earth, a large breast swollen with compassion's milk,
aches for all to drink.

Withdrawal

Darkness cannot be pulled from the night
nor heat from the sun.
And the tongue?
It is either honey or a club.
The way you hold it
or let syllables drip from its flesh.
And the way you swirl words in the river
of your mouth will make your tongue a boat.
How do you carry your greetings? Anger?
The tent of your love?
Not in the hands
or the luggage of your ribs,
but in the words you speak.
When you say them you cannot see them,
but the sound of them can lift or bow a head.

Genesis

After viewing Nocturne by Meg Reilly

One minute after midnight,
in the womb of darkness,
stars pour across the sky,
like rain
dripping their light into the canal of day.

On The Other Side, Almost

1

This pandemic season is an unpredictable harvest.
An increase here. A decrease there.
"Vaccine" is on the COVID menu.
Citizens still eat from a buffet of division.
The only "Post" I know is a brand of cereal.
I eat the *Honey Bunches of Wheat.*

2

A bulky bowl of black clouds rests on the table of sky.
I race past wheat-colored pastures on the way home.
Before hail and hard rain pinged on tarry streets,
I walked a looped mile where jackrabbits mated
in lofty coarse grass, my mask tucked in my pocket
like a crumpled receipt.

3

After slicing up my address, I crumple a stack
of unsolicited circulars, toss them in a wastebasket.
The bluff or their colorful annoyance crumbles to the floor
when I accidently kick the brown basket.
I scoop up the spill, mingle it with other trash,
trek to the dumpster, my name now a black trail
of crumbs ants cannot follow.

4

I sweep chip crumbs into my napkin. Forget
the waitress or the busboy I witnessed earlier
shoveling plates, glasses, and soiled silverware
into a gray tub will do it for me.
Six months since my vaccination, fourteen months
since I visited the insides of a restaurant.
Fear is a marauder.
My emotions run a marathon from anxiety to euphoria

as I fork chicken enchiladas. I have a desire to play
Marco Polo with other edgy guests but the sound
of the mariachi would drench their trembling voices.

5

I am drenched in anticipation as I wait
for lemon-colored canna lilies to open.
Childlike, I peek out the backdoor twice a day,
survey a corner of the yard congested with clusters
of my shrub roses' pink bountiful blooms.
Such assumption I have for their beauty.
Like the supposition I once had about this earth.
How it would rotate on its axis without glitches.
How air would remain chaste as truth.
Tomorrow is a string of pearls.
The past two weeks a sealed path of yesterdays.
Today I cup detached canna lily petals in my grateful hand.
Their yellow softness an answered prayer.
I track dried dirt through the kitchen
as the mourning doves coo-oo-oo song echoes
between new strands of hair creeping across
my chemoed bald head. I am on the other side,
almost.

How the Pandemic Has Changed the Way I Live

Life Lessons from Professor COVID

For the past year, COVID has dressed in inconvenience while masking itself as teacher. Often, I cursed the former. Now, I recognize the latter. I received my third cancer diagnosis in 2020, at the beginning of the pandemic, and am still in treatment. The lessons I have learned, my outlook, and the way I navigate the world are intertwined with healing and restrictions.

Lesson One: There are "no small things."

I am an introvert. Pre-COVID, there were times I would spend an entire weekend sequestered in my home, without even having a phone conversation. Nonetheless, I had the option to enter into the community at will. While putzing around town, whether a quick dash into the mall, dining out, grocery shopping, or standing in line at the movie theatre, it was common place to encounter both former and current students, as well as their parents. So often I was greeted with smiles larger than a full moon, and "Hi Miss Walker! What are you doing here?" Ah, the element of surprise. The very young students were mesmerized with the idea I engaged in activities outside that box of a building they knew as school. Students were especially excited to see me in restaurants, happy I did not always eat in the school cafeteria. Some of the most interesting conversations I had with them happened while standing in line at Walmart. Because those exchanges occurred frequently, I took them for granted. I did not realize the fullness of those encounters until I experienced the emptiness of not having them. This was also true of friends and acquaintances I had not seen for a while. As a result, when I was able to teach face-to-face again, I learned to appreciate my students' smiles and quirks more than before. I also became a note and card hoarder. Every card, note, letter I received via post, and from my students were housed in plastic containers. One of my favorite sacks is Rice Krispie Treats. A close friend purchased a box for me to carry to work and wrote a note on each treat. I have the empty wrappers saved in a plastic bag. Words became surrogates for the interaction I craved.

Lesson Two: Do it afraid.

I had no idea how often I accepted impromptu invitations for granted — to go for a walk, to a concert, to dinner, to see a movie, to take a day or weekend trip. I was clueless as to how much of my social life involved a quick bite before or get something after. I forgot the intimacy of sharing a meal. I returned to the classroom, face-to-face, in August of 2020. My oncologist had released me to return to work with the stipulations I wear a mask, shield, and practice social distancing when possible. I started the school term with anxiety sipping from my well-being. Less than a week into the semester, all personnel in the district were required to wear a mask, shield, and practice social distancing when inside the building. Students returned to school in phases and the older children were required to wear masks. These procedures were in place pre-vaccine and remained in place post-vaccine. The protocol eased my anxiety. From August to December, I ate lunch alone. My contact with other teachers was very limited. In January of 2021, I was fully vaccinated and started eating lunch with other staff members. However, it was weeks before I ventured into a restaurant. With every lunch or dinner invitation, I could feel anxiety clutching my stomach. The first time I walked into Jason's Deli, I could hardly breathe. It took me several minutes to settle down before I could eat. That was my inaugural moment of *doing something afraid*. With that experience, I accepted more lunch and dinner invitations, returned to some department stores, attended funerals, parties, and traveled outside of the county. This lesson is ongoing. Although I have been given permission by my oncologist to return to the gym, I have yet to do so — or to attend a concert. In those two areas, anxiety clamps its teeth in my whole being.

Lesson Three: Let Go. Forgive. Live.

One school cafeteria lady and her husband offered to gift me with a garden. Gardening is their passion. For several weeks I resisted, said thank you, but no thank you. When a friend asked, "Why don't you just let them do this for you?" I had to examine my motivation for saying no. I discovered it was about anger and control. I was angry because my body betrayed me, turned on itself, got sick after I did everything I could to prevent it. Control is the greatest illusionist I know. No matter how I cocooned myself, made plans, and worked the plans, life came along and unraveled everything I had so tightly stitched. Planting a garden properly was a simple act I could not physically do at the time they offered. As difficult as it was, I finally said yes. Not only did they plant my garden, they gave my mulberry a much-needed trim, raked leaves, relocated pavers, spruced up my side and backyards. After that gift acceptance, I learned to let others enter in places I kept so guarded. I started saying yes when others offered to bring dinner, lunch, an ice-cream treat, pick-up groceries, run errands, or help me in other ways. I honored my limitations. I had to let go of my past, the positive along with the negative, and accept what I could and could no longer do. I had to forgive my body for getting ill, then celebrate it for fighting to heal. I extended this forgiveness to my shortcomings and other areas of my life and to others who are no longer in my life. Some days I stand at my backdoor, peer through the screen, gaze at my garden, and smile. I snap photos, text them to my gardeners when a canna lily opens. That garden is a metaphor for my life. It is a gift, no matter what state it is in. Each day I remind myself: "Today is the tomorrow you hoped for."

Books by Loretta Diane Walker

Day Begins When Darkness Is in Full Bloom (Blue Light Press, 2021)

From the Cow's Eye and Other Poems (Fort Worth Poetry Society, 2021)

Ode to My Mother's Voice and Other Poems (Lamar University Literary Press, 2019)

Desert Light (Lamar University Literary Press, 2017)

In This House (Blue Light Press, 2016)

Word Ghetto (Blue Light Press, 2011)

Word Flirtations: Poems of the Everyday (Arlington Press, 2006)

About the Author

Loretta Diane Walker, a musician — tenor saxophonist, a daughter navigating a new world, a teacher who still likes her students, a two-time breast cancer survivor, and an artist who has been humbled and inspired by a collection of remarkable people and poets, is a member of the Texas Institute of Letters, a Best of the Net Nominee, a nine-time Pushcart Nominee and was named "Statesman in the Arts" by the Heritage Council of Odessa. Her collection *From the Cow's Eye and Other Poems* won the 2021 William D. Barney Memorial Chapbook Contest sponsored by the Fort Worth Poetry Society, her collection *In This House*, Blue Light Press, won the 2016 Phillis Wheatley Book Award and her manuscript *Word Ghetto* won the 2011 Blue Light Press Book Award. Loretta was the commencement speaker for the University of Texas at the Permian Basin graduation ceremonies in May of 2016. Her work has appeared in various literary journals, magazines, and anthologies throughout the United States, Canada, India, Ireland, and the UK. She has published seven collections of poetry. Loretta is a member of the Poetry Society of Texas, the National Federation of State Poetry Societies, The Permian Basin Poetry Society, Pennsylvania Poetry Society, Delta Sigma Theta Sorority, Inc., and is on the Public Art Advisory Committee of Odessa, Texas. She received a BME from Texas Tech University and earned a MA from The University of Texas of the Permian Basin. She teaches elementary music at Reagan Magnet School, Odessa, Texas.

Naomi Shihab Nye states, "Loretta Diane Walker writes with compassionate wisdom and insight — her poems restore humanity."

www.ingramcontent.com/pod-product-compliance
Lightning Source LLC
Chambersburg PA
CBHW022136080426
42734CB00006B/379